AF173895

HELLO BEES

THE POWERFUL POLLINATORS FOR OUR PLANET

Just imagine it's a hot summer day. You've just been swimming, and you're ready for lunch. What would you love to eat more than anything? I bet you said a nice, red, juicy piece of watermelon.

But did you know, without bees, there wouldn't be any watermelons? **It's true!**

Without bees, we also wouldn't have apples, peaches, blueberries, grapes, almonds, cashews, coffee, cucumbers, eggplants, and tangerines. And these are just a few of the many fruits, veggies, and nuts we wouldn't have if it weren't for bees!

But how is that possible? What do bees have to do with our food?

About 1/3 of the fruits, vegetables, and nuts we eat need bees to ***pollinate*** them. Pollinate is a fancy word for spreading pollen between individual plants and fertilizing them. Basically, by flying from plant to plant and collecting nectar and pollen, bees carry that pollen to other plants of that kind and let them be fertilized. This "pollination" allows plants to grow the vegetables, fruits, and nuts we love to eat.

ALL THINGS BEES FOR KIDS

FILLED WITH PLENTY OF FACTS, PHOTOS, AND FUN TO LEARN ALL ABOUT BEES

ANIMAL READS

WWW.ANIMALREADS.COM

THIS BOOK
BELONGS TO...

_____

_____

WWW.ANIMALREADS.COM

CONTENTS

Ever heard the term *"busy bee?"* There's a reason for that! Bees are extremely hard workers and stay busy pollinating plants their entire lives.

It's a good thing too!

WHAT IS A BEE?

Bees are flying insects whose main job is pollinating plants. Some kinds of bees make honey, like the Western honey bee, but the world of bees is so much more than just honey bees. **There are well over 16,000 different kinds, or species, of**

bees! This large group of species is ordered into 7 different bee "family groups." The most recognizable bee species, like the honey bee, fall into the Apidae group. But there are other bee groups for some other species, such as sweat bees, mining bees, leafcutter bees, and plasterer bees. We will explore them all a little later in this book!

WHAT IS SMALL, BLACK AND YELLOW, AND DROPS **THINGS?**

A fumble BEE!

ALL ABOUT THE LOOKS

CHARACTERISTICS AND APPEARANCE

I t's hard to mistake a bee! Few insects are as recognizable as these yellow and black-stripped, fuzzy friends. Actually, you may not know that honey bees are not black at all, but dark brown. They have dark brown bodies with yellow stripes. And some species of bees can look quite different, even metallic green or blue color patterns! So, just because it isn't black with yellow stripes, it could still be a bee.

Bees are insects. This means, like all other insects, they have a 3-part body and 6 legs. Their body is made up of their **head, thorax,** and **abdomen.** Bees are pretty wide compared to some insects. They are thick and hairy. The tiny hairs covering their bodies and legs help them collect the yellow pollen powder from the plants they visit.

External Anatomy of a Honey Bee

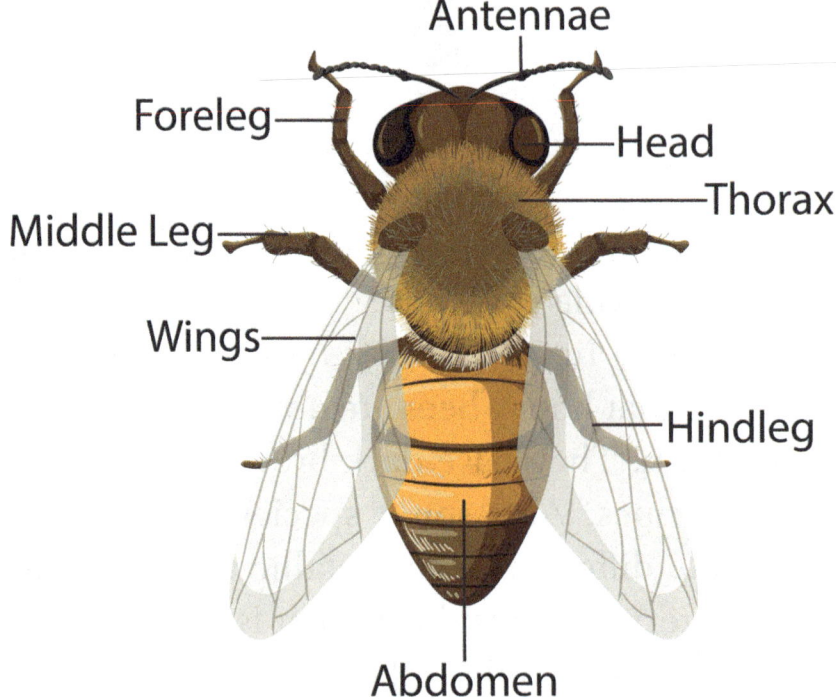

Bees range in size from the mosquito bee, a tiny species at just 3/50th of an inch, to carpenter bees that can be 1 ½ inches long. Honey bees are usually between ½ to 1 inch long.

Bees use their two pairs of wings to fly. Although they can fly really fast, they don't typically need to. Their average speed is around 12 miles per hour (20 kilometers). The typical "buzzing" sound you hear from a bee is actually the sound made from their wings.

For a bee, the most important thing is being able to find flowers for food. Flowers also need bees to carry their pollen to other flowers of their kind. Flowers attract bees by being colorful. Bees have 2 large eyes on the front of their head and 3 small eyes on the top. They can see every color you can see, except for red. Bees can also see types of light that you can't, such as ultraviolet light and polarized light. As red flowers reflect ultraviolet light very well, bees use this to find these flowers. Bees are also able to see movement and patterns/markings very well.

If you want to play some music for bees, you might be out of luck. Bees don't have any ears and can't hear the way we do. But they can feel vibrations from sounds when landing on sur-faces. *So, who knows?* **Maybe bees can hear it with their bodies after all!**

Another important sense for bees is their ability to smell. After all, flowers use beautiful scents to attract bees. Bees are very drawn to sweet smells, but bees don't have a nose like you do. Bees use their antennae, the feelers on top of their head, to "smell" their way to a sweet flower nectar lunch. Once they find food, bees use their ***proboscis*** (*a kind of tongue/mouth/tube*) to suck up nectar and eat. They also have ***mandibles***, which are *claw-like jaws* to grab things with. Bees are very good at telling if food is sweet, bitter, sour, or salty.

If you've ever looked closely at a bumblebee, you'll know that bees are pretty hairy. *But this*

cute fuzz isn't just for looks. The hairs covering a bee's body and legs serve an important role. As the bee lands on flowers, the yellow pollen dust sticks to these hairs.

The bee then flies to another flower and collects pollen from that plant as well, while also rubbing off pollen from previous flowers it has visited. This is what we call "***pollination***," *the spreading of one plant's pollen with another.* This allows plants to be fertilized and to create fruit, vegetables, and nuts.

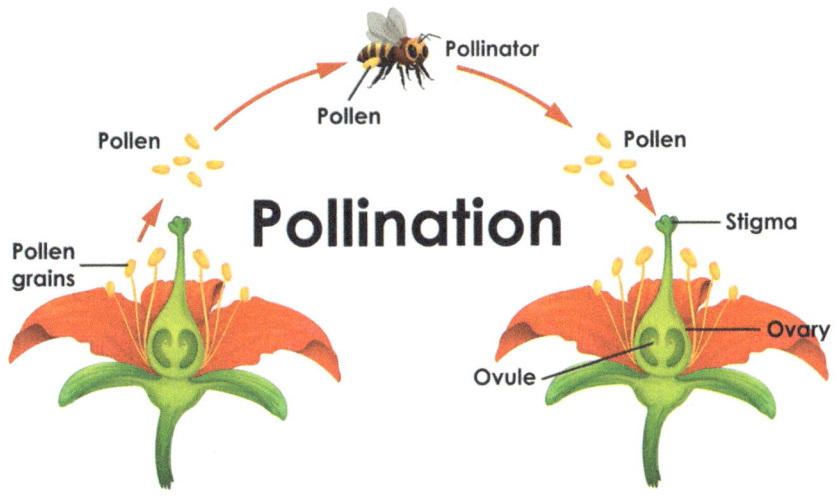

FLOWERS: NATURE'S PERFECT FOOD FOR BEES

Bees spend a great deal of their life looking for food. Bees visit 100's of flowers a day, collecting nectar and pollen.

Nectar is the sweet liquid made by flowers. Remember how bees have a long proboscis, a kind of mouth tube? They stick this into the flower and suck out the nectar, which they hold in a special part of their stomach. For honey bees, this nectar mixes with enzymes and becomes honey. The worker bee will then return to the hive and *regurgitate* (*bring back up*) the liquid honey and place it into a honeycomb chamber. The honey is left to thicken, and when it is just right, the bee will create a wax cap to close off the chamber and keep the honey from drying out. *This is important because guess what bees eat all winter when there are no more flowers around and no nectar to be found?* **That's right! Honey.**

Honey is the bee's way of preserving food, so the hive can survive all winter long.

Bees also eat pollen, which they collect from the flowers and plants they visit. While sugary nectar gives the bees lots of energy, pollen provides them with protein and other nutrients they need for a complete diet. Honey bees also combine honey and pollen into little balls to create "*bee bread*." Bee bread is a super-nutritious food that is rich in protein and fed to young bees.

IS IT A BEE, WASP, OR HORNET?

While there are differences between bees, wasps, and hornets, they do share a few things in common. All three of these insects can sting. All of them live in hives or shelters that they make themselves. They also can look similar. Many species are striped with yellow and black markings. Although some wasps and hornets can also be other colors like red or brown.

ATTITUDE SAYS IT ALL

Probably the largest difference between bees and wasps/hornets is their attitude. While bees are industrious workers, minding their own business and more interested in collecting pollen than bothering you or your watermelon slice, wasps and hornets are another story.

Wasps are predators and can be pretty hostile and relentless in going after a good meal. The end of their body is pointy and looks like you put a belt on a bee and cinched it as tight as it would go! Their skinny waists and long bodies are one of the ways you can tell them apart from bees, as well as their tendency to hover around your picnic and not leave you alone.

FAT AND FUZZY OR SLIM AND SLEEK?

Unlike fuzzy bees, wasps have a very sleek appearance with almost no hair on their bodies. This makes sense because they don't need to collect pollen from plants like honey bees and bumblebees do. Wasps don't have much to do with pollinating plants. Wasps are hunters, and they build nests to shelter in. They eat fruit, human food, plants, and other insects like bees, flies, larva, and caterpillars. Near the end of the summer, wasps tend to get more aggressive as they look for food. If you've ever had a wasp buzzing around your ice cream cone, this is why. They don't like to take no for an answer and can be very persistent in going after food.

JUST WHEN YOU THOUGHT WASPS COULD GET NO WORSE!

If wasps sound bad, wait until you meet hornets! A lot of people think hornets are their own group entirely, but they are actually a type of wasp. Hornets are almost super wasps—more venomous and sometimes larger. Giant species of hornets, like the "*murder hornet*," whose real name is the giant Asian hornet, can be 2 inches long, and just a handful can easily kill an entire honey bee colony! However, you'll be glad to know honey bees are not entirely defenseless to these giant bee-killers.

Japanese honey bees have adapted to protect themselves from giant Asian hornets. If a hornet scout comes to the hive, the honey bees will surround the hornet in a swarm. By doing so, they create a ball of bees around the enemy. By combining their bodies together, the bees raise the temperature inside the ball and close the hornet inside the heat. Carbon dioxide also builds up within the ball, and the combination of this with the heat kills the hornet scout before it can return to its group and report on the hive's location.

WHAT DO YOU CALL A WASP?

A wanna BEE!

SO MANY BEES

Now that you know the bee world is full of many kinds of bees, let's take a look at some of the best known and most fascinating species around today.

HONEY BEE

The most famous and well-loved of all bees is the Honey bee. Honey bees live in nests or homes, which are called **hives.** They can have around 25,000 bees in their colony. Each honey bee visits hundreds of flowers a day to collect nectar and pollen. Honey bees have a special kind of hair on their rear legs that acts like Velcro to pollen. A honey bee can carry its own weight in pollen.

Worker bees that collect nectar use this sweet liquid to create honey. The honey liquid is then stored in wax chambers, which you are probably familiar with. We call these "honeycombs." After 5 days, the mixture thickens and now resembles honey. This honey is then covered with a thin layer of wax to store it for later use.

BUMBLEBEE

Another easily recognizable species of bee is the bumblebee. These fat, hairy foragers are almost double the size of honey bees and are hard to miss in the garden as they "bumble" along. They are slow and pretty friendly. If you leave a bumblebee alone, it won't bother you. Bumblebees tend to have wide bands of yellow on their black bodies. Sometimes they have a red, orange, or white tail. Unlike honey bees, bumblebees live in small colonies of only a few hundred members. Bumblebees usually make their nest somewhere underground, although they sometimes make nests in walls or holes other animals created.

CARPENTER BEE

The carpenter bee gets its name for its love of wood. These bees drill holes into posts, trees, or even your house! The tell-tale sign of a carpenter bee is a small pile of sawdust on the ground below a small hole. The bees create their nest within the hole that they dig out.

As most people don't like their fences or decks full of small holes, carpenter bees are often considered pests. Carpenter bees are large and look similar to bumblebees. One way to tell them apart is their abdomen. If their lower half is shiny and all black, it's probably a carpenter bee. Bumblebees are fuzzy all over and have a yellow stripe. Carpenter bees are solitary bees and do not live in a colony or large group.

SWEAT BEE

Sweat bees are actually an entire category of bees called the Halictidae group. This group of bees is one of the largest, with around 4,500 different species within it. These bees are typically brown

or black and look slightly metallic. Another popular color for sweat bees is green, and some
species can even be purple or blue. This group
gets its popular name of "sweat bee" because
these bees seem to be drawn to sweaty, salty skin.
But don't worry, these bees aren't aggressive, and
only the females can sting. If you find, on a hot
summer day, that a sweat bee has landed on your
arm, it's probably just getting a quick taste of the
salt on your skin. Some of the tiniest bees are
part of this group.

KILLER BEE

**Yikes! Nobody wants to hear there are killer
bees around!** These bees are actually called
Africanized honey bees, and they are a hybrid

breed that was created by accident. 26 swarms (*or hives*) of the East African lowland honey bee were being kept in Brazil, and they escaped. These African bees went on to cross-breed with other honey bee species and created a hybrid bee.

These bees are much more reactive than typical honey bees. Because they respond more aggressively to any perceived threat, killer bee attacks can be really dangerous. The bees sting ten times more than a typical bee would. Sadly, they have killed horses and livestock, and even some people.

While the term "*killer bee*" can sound scary, it actually doesn't tell the whole story. It's true that Africanized honey bees are more reactive to disturbances to their hive and may sting more than a typical bee. However, their stings are not any worse than a regular bee sting, and they do not go out seeking to sting people or animals. They actually only want to get their work done without being disturbed.

MINING BEE

Mining bees are great at tunneling into the dirt. They create a nest underground that consists of a long hallway, with short *"doors"* leading off into small cells called "nursery cells." These chambers are where the mining bee leaves nectar and an egg. The eggs will grow into the next generation of miners. The mining bee lines the hallways with clay and water that it spits up.

LEAFCUTTER BEE

Leafcutter bees are solitary bees, which means they work and live alone. They build a small nest within a hollow space like a hole in the ground or a rotted-out piece of wood. They get their name from the unusual habit of cutting circles out of leaves from shrubs and bushes. The leafcutter bee will take these circles and build small compartments to lay an egg in. They deposit one egg, some food, and then seal the chamber with another leaf circle. This creates a safe place for the growing larva to develop and the cycle to continue.

WHAT GOES ZZUB-ZZUB WHEN IT TRAVELS?

A bee flying backwards!

A HISTORY OF BEES

In the history of the natural world, bees have been around for nearly 65 million years. Bees seem to have evolved from hunting wasps that preyed on other insects. But unlike their carnivorous ancestors, bees developed to eat pollen and nectar, not other insects.

The oldest known fossil of a bee is from the mid-Cretaceous period. This fossil was found in New Jersey in a hunk of amber, which is fossilized tree resin. This fossil shows some kind of "corbiculate" bee, which is the same family as honey bees and bumblebees.

One theory of why bees evolved to eat pollen instead of prey is that perhaps the bees first ate flower-dwelling bugs, or fed these bugs to their young. It's possible that these "food" bugs were covered in pollen and led to the development of eating pollen as well.

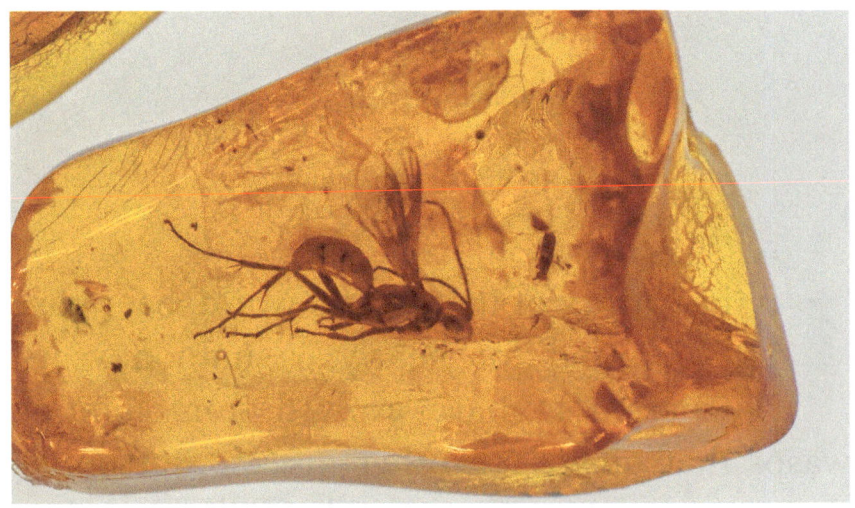

Scientists are also exploring the idea that the switch from insect food to flower food might be connected to the arrival of many kinds of flowering plants in the mid-Cretaceous period. This broadening of the types of foods bees could now eat might explain why so many different species of bees started to show up around this time period as well.

I'M **JUST WINGING IT!**

WHERE DO WE LIVE?

As long as there are flowering plants, you will find bees! Bees live in every part of the world except Antarctica. And it's a good thing too. As chief pollinators of the world's plants and crops, bees are an important part of every ecosystem on earth.

SOCIAL BEES: COLONY/HIVE-DWELLERS

The most well-known and popular bee in the world is probably the honey bee. Honey bees live in hives and have colonies made up of several thousand members. These bees are considered "social" bees because they live all together in a society with rules, jobs, and order. A honey bee colony is made up of three types of bees—the **queen**, the **workers**, and the **drones.**

Drone   Queen   Worker

THE QUEEN

As you might have guessed, the queen is in charge. She is quite a bit larger than the other honey bees, and her one job is to lay eggs. **She lays around 1500 eggs a day and will lay almost 1 million eggs in her lifetime of 2-3 years.**

The Queen

The queen also produces special scents, called *pheromones*, that send messages to the bees. These scent messages tell the bees how to behave and even keeps the other females in the group from maturing into queens themselves.

THE WORKERS

The next group in the colony is the workers. Workers make up the largest part of the bee community by far, and they are all female. These are the only bees you are likely to see as they are the ones who go out and collect nectar and pollen. They also care for young bees, build the hive, make the honey, and do all the work of the colony. In the busy Spring and Summer seasons, worker bees only live around 5 to 6 weeks. However, in the winter, workers can live for 4 to 6 months.

THE DRONES

The last group of bees that make up the colony is the drones. For every few thousand worker bees, there are only about 100 drones. Drones are males who have the sole job of mating with the queen. As they often die in the mating process or right afterward, they typically only live for around 2 weeks.

You might think that the honey bees would feel bad to have such a short life. But thankfully, they don't. For honey bees, everything they do is about helping the hive and the community to survive. They are truly selfless workers, doing everything they can for the betterment and survival of the colony.

SOLITARY BEES: ON THEIR OWN

Most people associate bees with "bee hives" or colonies where the bees live together and work for the good of the hive. If you asked the average person where bees live, I bet most would say, *"Bees live in a bee hive with other bees."* But, aside from honey bees and bumblebees, they would be wrong!

Bees who don't live in a giant hive or colony are called "solitary" bees. This means they live alone.

Most bees are actually solitary bees. Out of the 16,000 different types of bees, about 90% (or 14,400) of bee species are solitary bees.

So, if these solitary bees don't live in a colony, where do they live? Solitary bees build nests in holes in the ground or empty cracks in wood or trees.

Solitary bees don't make honey, so all they need is a small quiet hole to rest in at the end of a hard day's work, raise their young, and a place to keep safe from predators. Solitary bees are much more individualistic than social bees. Their focus is solely on providing for their own needs and raising a few offspring to take their place. Female solitary bees usually live around 6 weeks, and males live around 2 weeks. These bees will typically raise around 25 offspring in their short lifetime.

WHEN DO BEES GET MARRIED?

When they've found their honey!

THE SHORT BUT SWEET LIFE CYCLE OF A BEE

L et's take a moment to explore the life cycle of a honey bee. In a honey bee colony, there is only one mother... for everyone! This special bee is called the queen. Have you ever looked at a picture of a bee hive or a piece of honeycomb? A bee hive is made up of lots of little pockets or "cells." These act like little rooms for storing all kinds of things, and the queen lays her eggs in cells. She deposits one egg per cell.

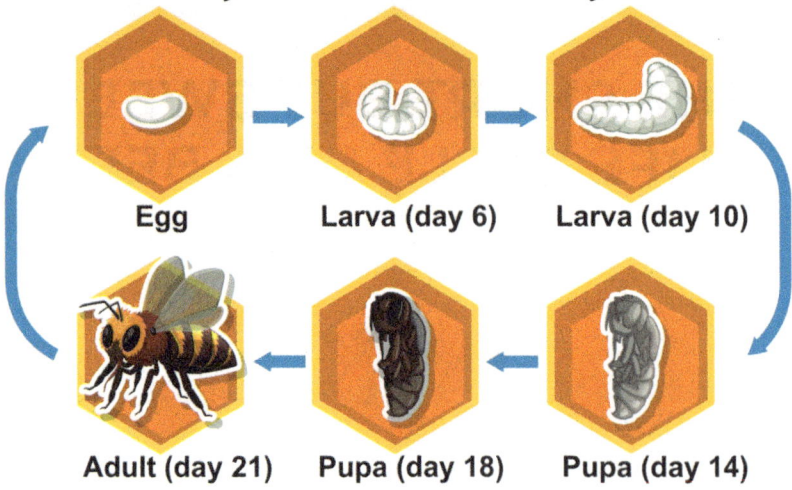

Egg   Larva (day 6)   Larva (day 10)

Adult (day 21)   Pupa (day 18)   Pupa (day 14)

FROM EGG TO FULL-GROWN BEE

A few days later, the egg grows into a larva, which looks like a little white grub. The larva's cell is then filled about halfway with a white liquid that is a special pool of food "*soup*." A group of female worker bees have the job of feeding and caring for the baby bees. The larva will lay in this soup and **eat** and **eat** and **eat**, and grow at a remarkable pace.

When it is large enough, the larva will spin a **cocoon** around itself and become a **pupa**. It will stay in the cocoon and grow for around 2 weeks before becoming a full-grown bee. At this time, the bee will climb its way out of the cell. All in all, the entire process from egg to bee takes around 3 weeks.

This process, raising eggs to grown bees, is a constant part of the work of the hive. As the average worker bee only lives from 3 weeks to a few months in the winter, the need for new bees is a constant one. Constantly raising new bees is the only way the hive can survive.

With such an efficient bee factory, you may be wondering if the bees ever out-grow their space. *Do they worry about creating too many*

bees? **Sometimes this does happen!** When there are too many bees for the space of their hive, the bees will get ready to split the colony in two. The queen will take half the colony and set out to find a new hive.

Since the queen is skilled at giving off different scents, she uses a special smell that tells the bees to follow her. The bees close enough to the queen will smell her scented signal and leave with her to create a new colony. Usually, this new group, or "swarm," is around a few thousand bees. *Imagine coming across that traveling caravan of bees in the sky!*

When the queen finds a place to land, the swarm of workers circle around her and cover her up to keep her safe. They then find food and look for a new place to make a hive. If they can't find a new place fast enough, they may die.

The remaining bees left at the old hive now have the task of growing some new queens. They will grow around 12 queens and choose a new leader from this group.

YOU ARE WHAT YOU EAT

You may be wondering, *with thousands of eggs hatching every day, how do the workers know which larvae will turn into queens?* **Actually, any larva can become a queen.** You know the term, *"You are what you eat?"* This is supposed to make us think about the kinds of food we put into our bodies. **Healthy food = a healthy body. Junk food = feeling junky or bad.**

But bees take the phrase "You are what you eat" to a whole new level. Queen bees are created from regular larvae, which are fed a special food called *"Royal jelly."* This is a milk-colored goo that literally creates queens. By eating this, these regular grubs will turn into queen bees!

Life for a bee is short but sweet. If a predator like a wasp or a swallow doesn't catch them, a worker bee can live out its life of around 30 days doing what it loves—working hard and giving everything for the hive, collecting nectar and pollen, pollinating plants, and ensuring the continuation of their kind.

WHAT DOES A BEE USE TO STYLE ITS HAIR?

A honey comb!

AWESOME FACTS ABOUT BEES

DID YOU KNOW?

- Bees have little areas of special hair on their legs which they use as pockets to hold pollen. This is kind of like when you wear cargo pants.

- Just one bee visits 100's of flowers in a single day!

- Honey bees go back to the hive once an hour to drop off their goods before going out to collect more.

- Did you know honey bees can dance? They do something called the waggle dance. When a worker bee finds a new food source, it returns to the hive and tells other bees where to find food. It gives directions by doing the waggle dance. The dancing bee will shake its body, spin, and make sounds.

- It takes nectar from about 2 million flowers to create 1 pound of honey! Each honey bee will only make around 1/12 of a teaspoon of honey in its whole life.

YOU'RE

THE BEES KNEES!

BEES NEED YOUR HELP

We hope you enjoyed learning all about bees and how these fuzzy friends help keep the world blooming and thriving! By now, we're sure you'll agree bees are super important, and we should do all we can to ensure these pollinators survive and thrive for years to come.

Before you decide how you can help, let's take a look at the threats and dangers facing bees today.

PESTICIDES

Nobody likes pulling weeds and grass out of cracks in the driveway or sidewalk. It's no wonder that pesticides have become so popular. Just one spray, and **BAM!** No more weeds to deal with. No more grass growing where it shouldn't.

But the problem is, pesticides like these and others are not only dangerous to our own health, they harm pollinators like bees. Some pesticides give bees a kind of memory loss, which causes them to be unable to remember where they belong and to abandon their hives. Pesticides have been shown to be fatal to pollinators, and many countries in the world have already banned the use of these chemicals to help save bees.

CLIMATE CHANGE

As the climate changes, bees have not gone unharmed. Wacky temperature changes have an effect on all of us! Flowers are also affected. If it is suddenly colder than normal, or hotter than normal, plants bloom or fail to bloom, which can put them out of sink with the bees and other pollinators who rely on these flowers and plants for food.

HOW CAN YOU HELP?

Now that you know just how important bees are to the world and the threats they face, what can you do to help?

Helping bees isn't hard! Here are a few things you can do to help ensure these important pollinators are around for the years to come:

THE FRIEND OF BEES ACTION PLAN

Speak Out Against Pesticides

Tell your grandpa, grandma, mom, dad, uncle, and anybody you can about the dangers of pesticides and lawn chemicals for bees and their pollinating friends. Offer to help weed or research green and earth/pollinator-friendly choices for getting rid of weeds and other lawn problems.

Create a Bee-Friendly Park in Your Yard

Pollinators need flowering weeds and plants. Can you section off a small area of your yard and set up a bee zone? Maybe you can make a small stick fence around it and make a sign to tell neighbors and passersby what it's for. Your bee park can grow clover, dandelions, wildflowers, or other native plants to your area that bees love. And hey, maybe your parents will even help! It means less area they have to mow. Your bee park can not only serve as a healthy, pesticide-free place for bees to find food, but it can also serve as a way to teach others in your community about the importance of bees.

Make Green Choices for a Healthy Planet

Every green, earth-friendly choice you make also helps bees. By recycling, saving energy, using less gas and oil, and avoiding the use of chemicals (both outdoors and inside), we all help to heal the planet that is home to bees and ourselves.

Will you be a friend to bees and tell the world how amazing these hard-working helpers are? We hope so!

EVERYTHING WILL
BEE OKAY!

THANK YOU!

Thank you for reading this book and for allowing us to share our love for bees with you!

If you've enjoyed this book, please let us know by leaving a rating and a brief review wherever you made your purchase! This helps us spread the word to other readers!

Thank you for your time, and have an awesome day!

For more information, please visit:

www.animalreads.com

WHAT DO BEES CHEW?

BUMBLE Gum!

© Copyright 2022 - All rights reserved Admore Publishing

ISBN: 978-3-96772-109-6

ISBN: 978-3-96772-110-2

Animal Reads at www.animalreads.com

The content contained within this book may not be reproduced, duplicated or transmitted without direct written permission from the author or the publisher.

Under no circumstances will any blame or legal responsibility be held against the publisher, or author, for any damages, reparation, or monetary loss due to the information contained within this book. Either directly or indirectly.

Published by Admore Publishing: Gotenstraße, Berlin, Germany

www.admorepublishing.com

Made in the USA
Monee, IL
05 August 2024

63256934R00044